DESIGN SOURCE BOOK FOR CRAFTERS

Judy Balchin
Courtney Davis
Polly Pinder
Mandy Southan

SEARCH PRESS

FLOWER DESIGNS

Mandy Southan

Flowers are one of the best loved subjects for decorative work. They have inspired artists and craftspeople through the ages and flower designs are as popular today as ever. Flowers make beautiful designs both when depicted realistically and in decorative, stylised ways. In my own work as a textile designer and silk painter, I find them a constant source of inspiration and they are always a favourite subject with my students.

Use the flower motifs as they are or make several copies and stick them together to form a pattern. There are borders, repeating panels and designs for items such as cushion covers, cards or wall hangings. When planning your craft work, you might like to look at real flowers or good photographs to give you ideas for colours and textures.

CELTIC DESIGNS

Courtney Davis

Many of the patterns within this section are based on Hiberno-Saxon designs created in Britain and Ireland from the 6th to the 12th century. They can be found carved in stone and on fine decorative church metalwork, elaborate jewellery and the highly illuminated pages of the Gospel books. Patterns such as the spiral and knotwork were not the invention of Celtic artisans, but were some of the first symbols used by humans to express their spirituality and the wonder of the world around them. It is the skill and imagination of Celtic and Saxon artists who took these patterns and adapted them, creating intricate and complex designs that still inspire us today — in works such as the Books of Kells and Lindisfarne and the Cross of Cong.

TRADITIONAL JAPANESE DESIGNS

Polly Pinder

Japanese design has been influenced by many cultures, notably Chinese, Korean, Indian and Persian, through hundreds of years of invasion, wars and trading. Eventually the influences became completely absorbed and helped to develop original Japanese expression. Symbols, emblems and pictorial images were used to embellish anything from a simple tea bowl to a paper umbrella.

Every period in Japan's history has produced its own distinct artistic style. During the Kamakura period (1185–1338) the military class, or samurai, developed simple designs with subtle colouring to decorate their armour. Later, during the Momoyama period (1573–1603) the kimono — the loose-fitting traditional Japanese dress — became a beautiful art form. Intricately woven, brocaded or embroidered fabrics were used, as were plain fabrics which were tie or stencil dyed to produce elaborate motifs.

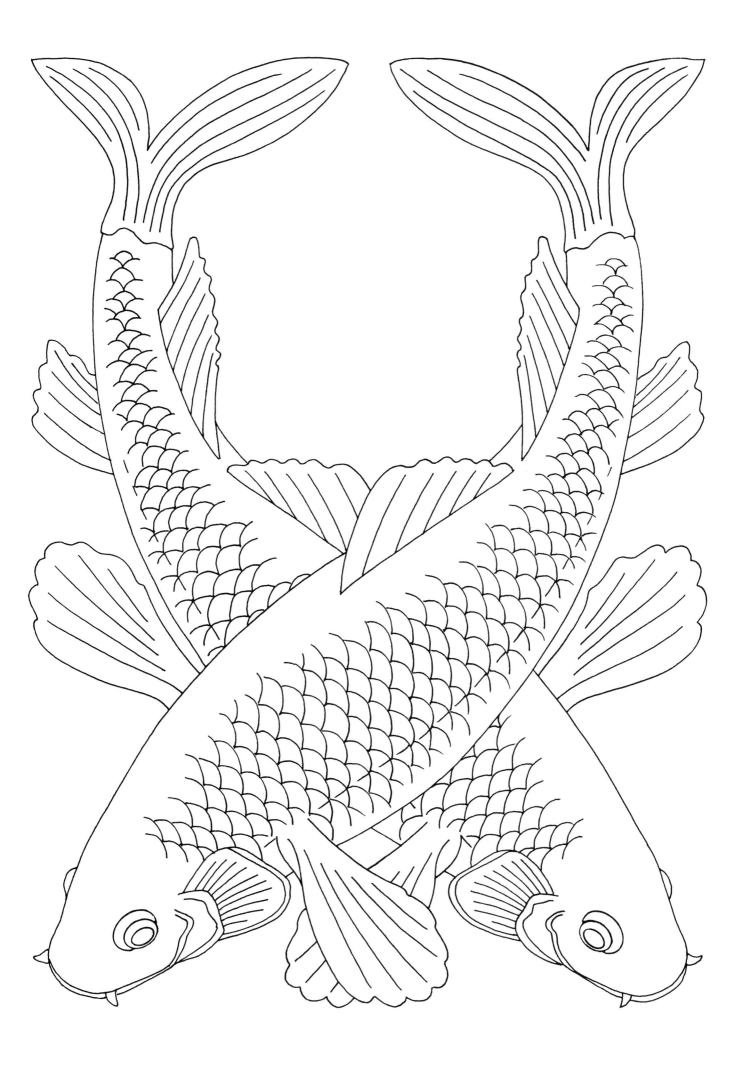

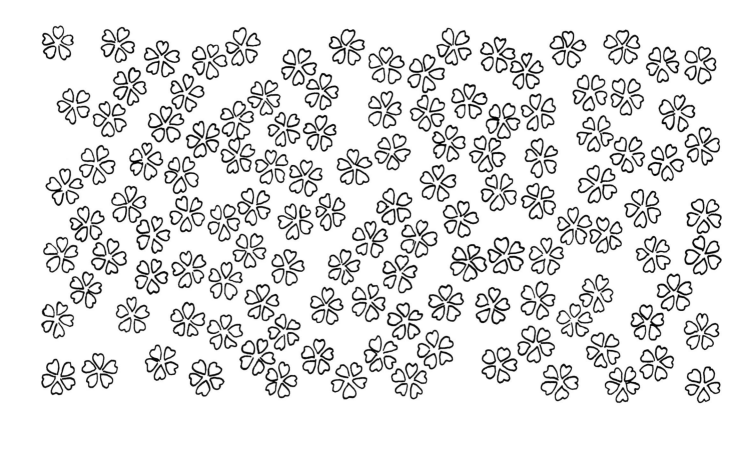

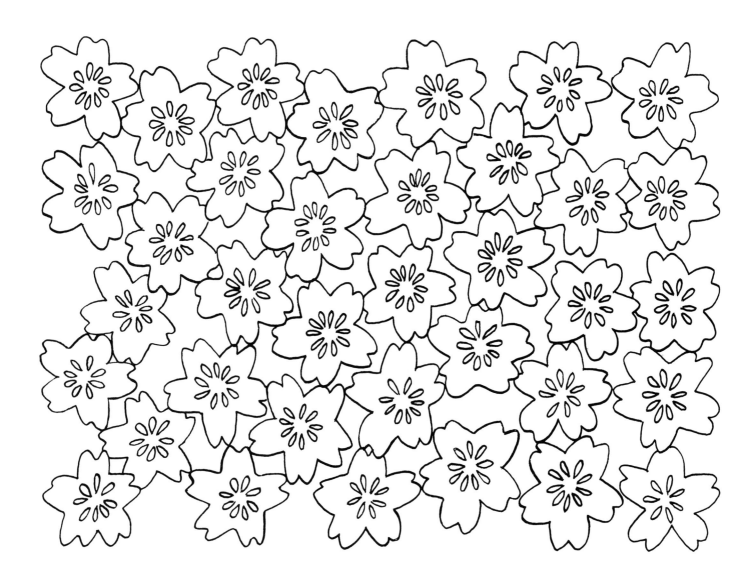

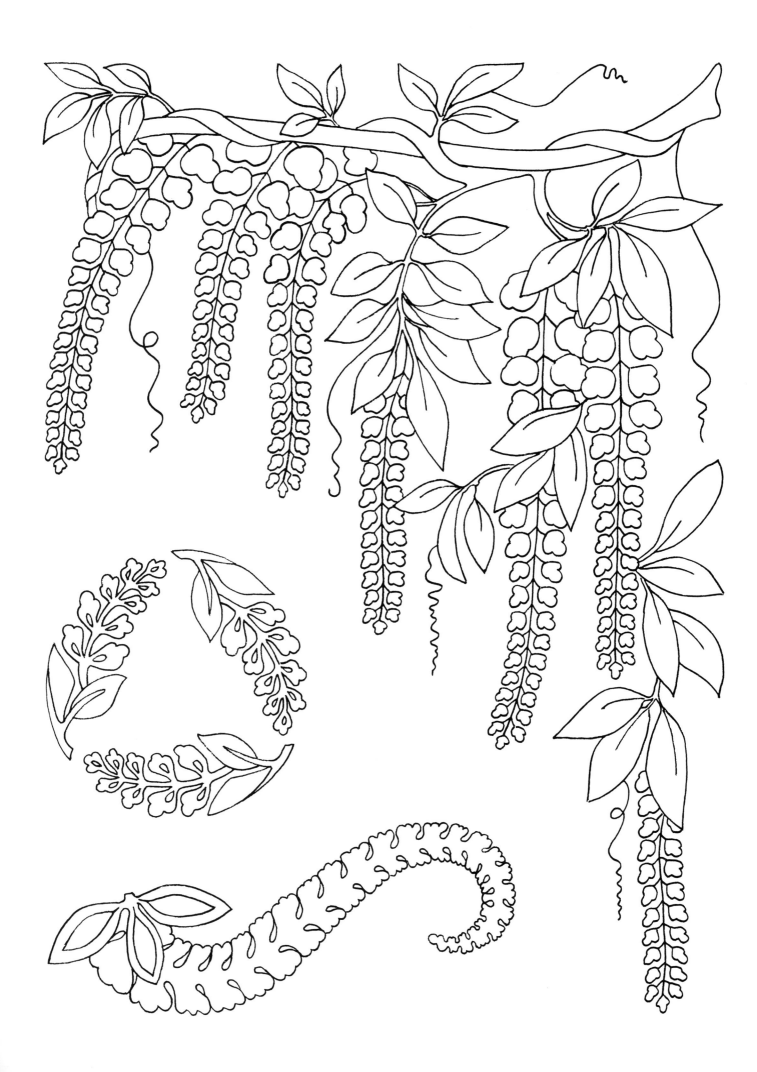

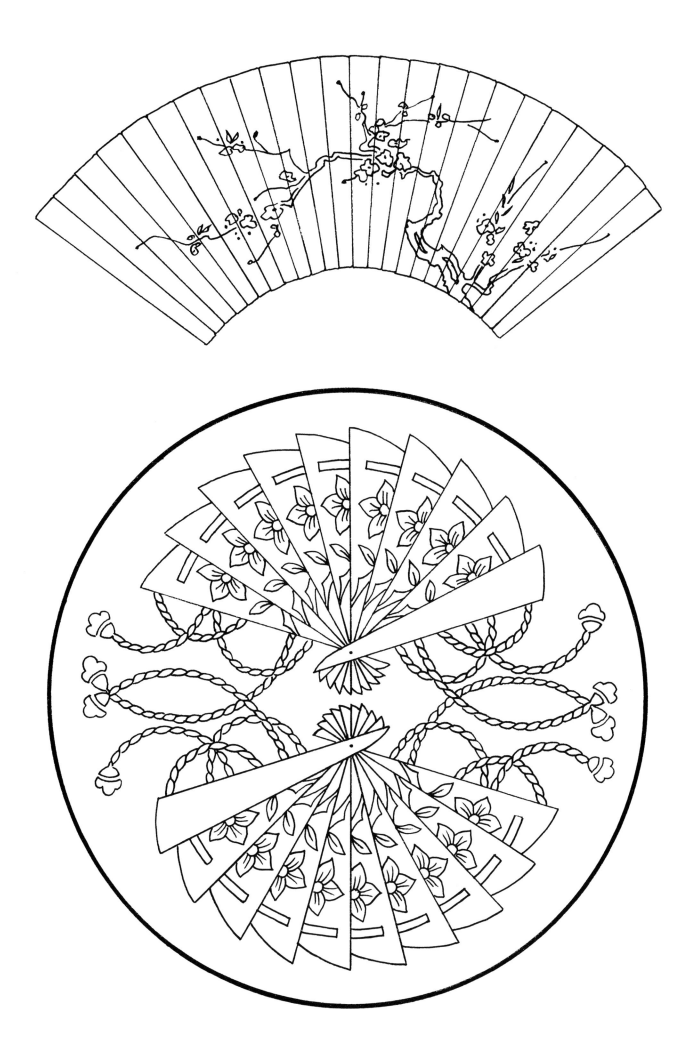

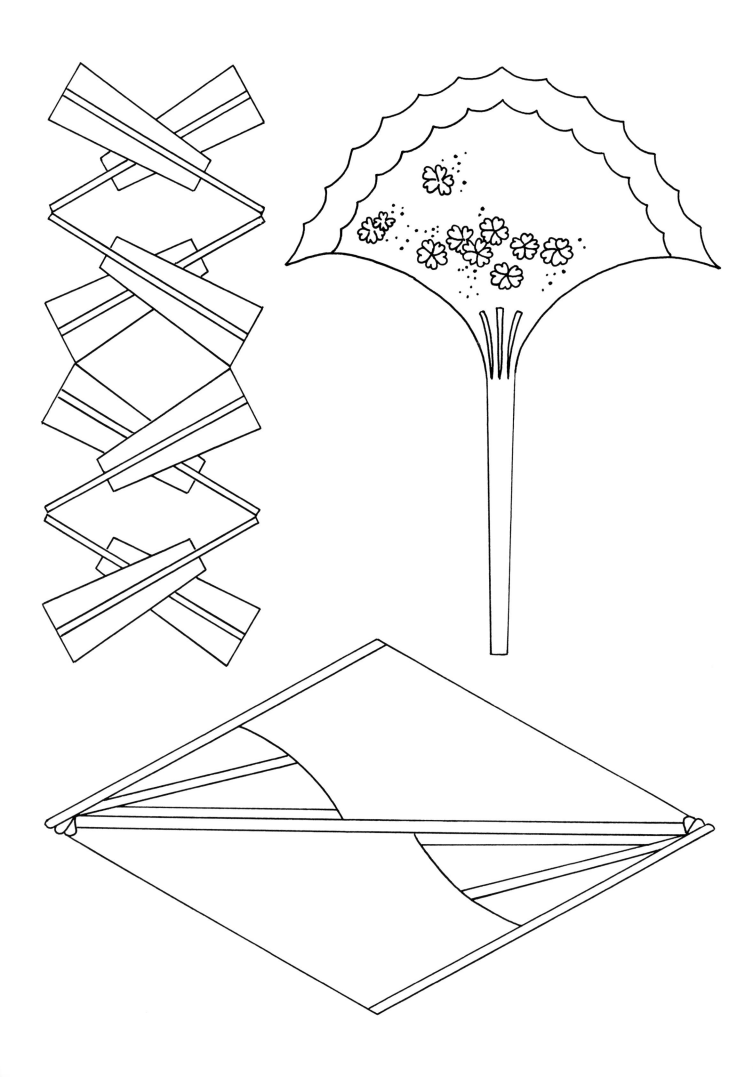

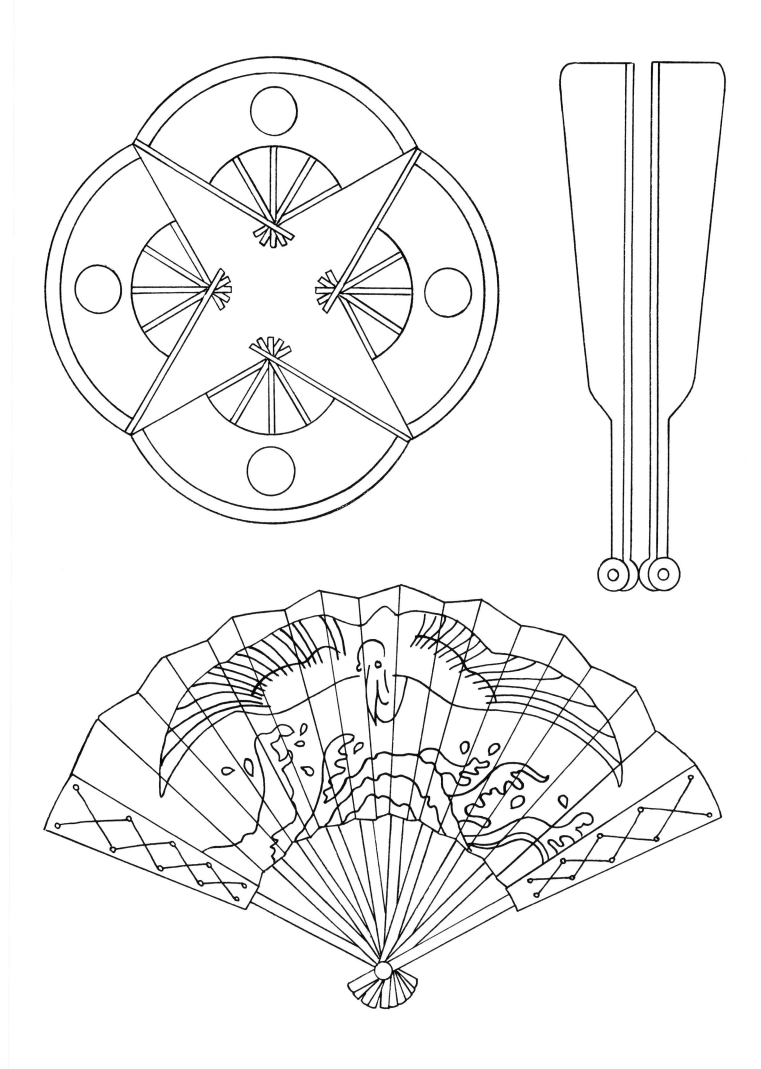

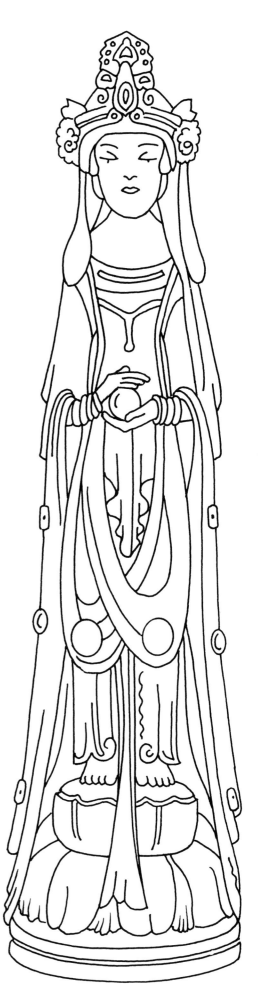

ART NOUVEAU DESIGNS

Judy Balchin

Art Nouveau developed in the 1880s and lasted in its purest form for a mere decade. Artists were mainly inspired by nature during this period, and a wonderful selection of floral and plant designs were interpreted with stylized, flowing lines. This graphic representation, where artists' lines seem almost fluid as they twine and curve over different surfaces, has left us with a wealth of beautifully organic designs to work from. The grace and freedom of the period offer us a huge range of classic designs which can be applied to numerous arts and crafts. Glass, silk and ceramic painters will be inspired by the patterns within this book — and so will needleworkers and decorative painters. In fact, anyone seeking a basic design to work from will find them useful as a starting point from which they can develop their own ideas. Your creativity will really come into play when you choose the colour combinations within the designs — something that I find my students excel at.

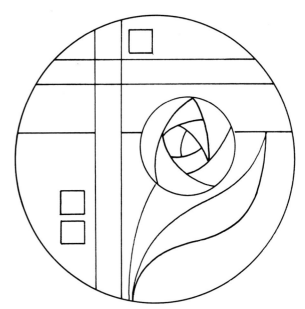

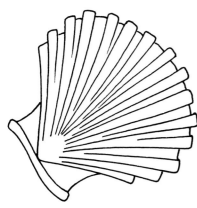

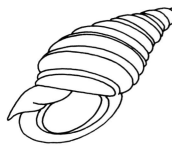

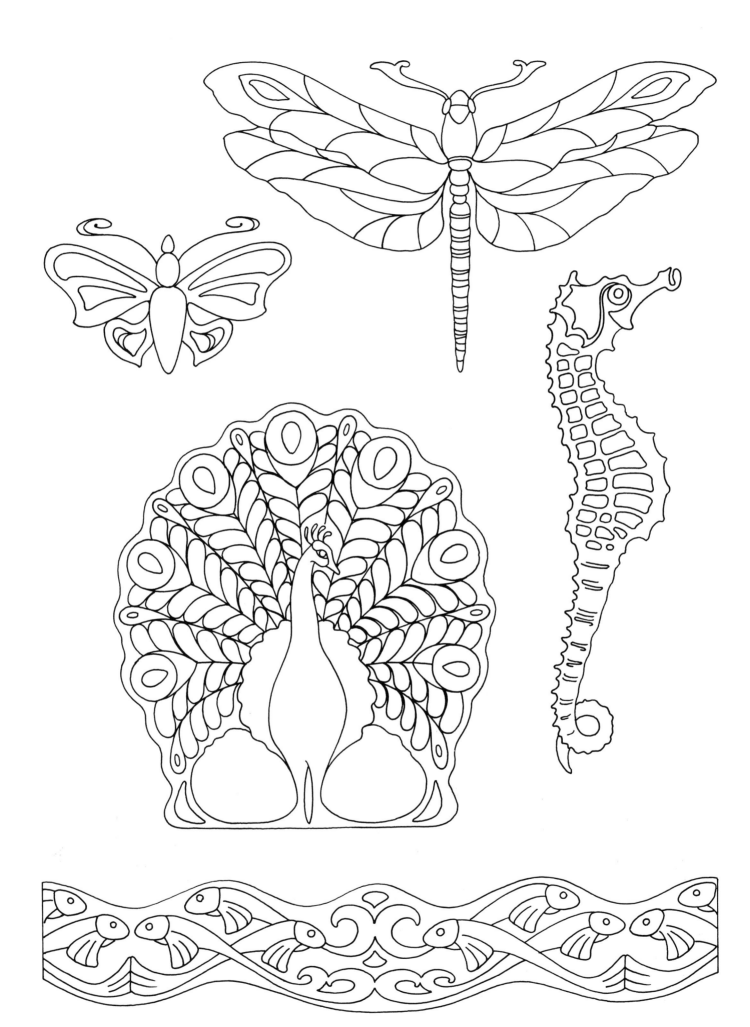

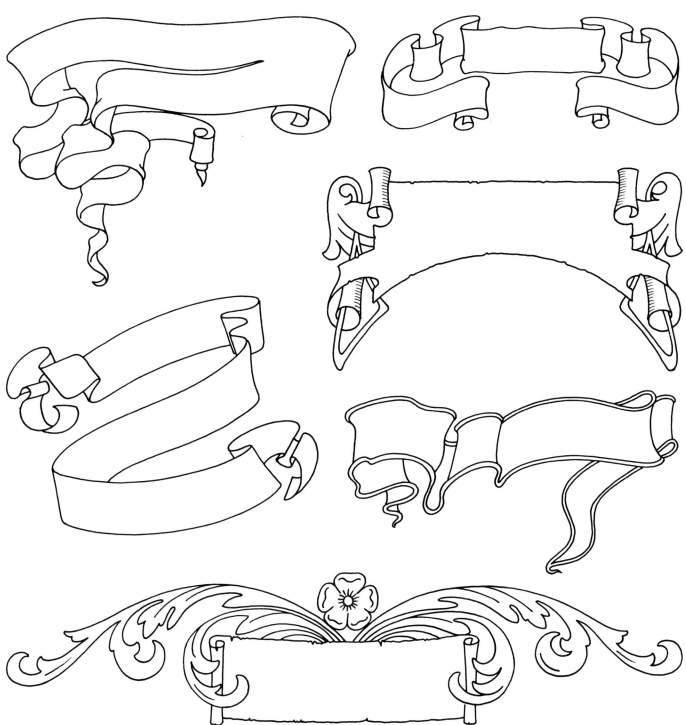

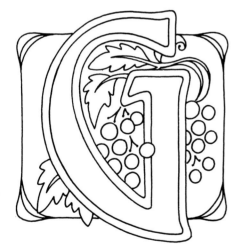

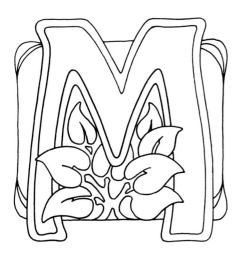

First published in Great Britain 2002

Search Press Limited, Wellwood, North Farm Road, Tunbridge Wells, Kent TN2 3DR

Copyright © Search Press Ltd. 2002

ISBN 1 903975 36 0